EARLY LEARNING EXPERIENCES IN CREATIVE ARTS

by Imogene Forte and Joy MacKenzie

Incentive Publications, Inc.
Nashville, Tennessee

Illustrated by Gayle Seaberg Harvey
Cover Design by Marta Drayton
Edited by Leslie Britt

ISBN 0-86530-295-2

PRINTED IN THE UNITED STATES OF AMERICA

Table Of Contents

About This Book . . .

Early Learning Experiences in Creative Arts has been planned to help young children learn through experimentation, through creative involvement in directed activities, and finally, through the joy of discovery.

Young children are curious about and extremely sensitive to their environment. They instinctively push and pull, take apart and attempt to put together again, smell, taste, feel, and listen to things around them. "Why?" "What?" "When?" "Where?" and "How?" are words they use naturally and often. It is this interaction with their environment that parents and teachers can either nurture and encourage or inhibit and retard. Children who have had many happy, satisfying opportunities to use their hands, feet, eyes, ears, and whole bodies are much more apt to adjust happily and successfully to more structured learning experiences.

The purpose of the activities in *Early Learning Experiences in Creative Arts* is to help children understand and appreciate their environment, to develop self-awareness, and to express themselves creatively.

The book includes a mix of simple hands-on activities, free choice activities, and more structured teacher-directed activities. While instructions are directed to the child, an adult will, of course, need to read and interact with the child in the interpretation and completion of the activities. Ideally, the projects will be presented in a stress-free setting that will afford time for the child to question, explore, wonder, ponder, and create—and to develop an abiding, imaginatively inquisitive approach to creative self-expression. The fanciful illustrations will provide added incentive for lively interaction. Each activity is intended to contribute to the development of skills and concepts which will enhance the child's self-concept and serve as a guide to personal achievement.

So . . . You've Invited A Winged Rhinoceros To Lunch!

What Will You Have To Eat?

Rattlesnake soup
And salad tossed high
With oil of white walrus
And bald eagle eye?

Or the warts of a toad
On bread lightly toasted
With lily-pad gravy
Over worms slightly roasted?

Maybe crocodile stew,
Lightly seasoned with snail
And puree of parrot
Served by the pail?

Or filet of fried falcon,
Garnished wings of a fly,
Steamed web-foot of duckling
And pelican pie!

Make up a pretend menu for your favorite imaginary animal friend. Ask someone to write it for you. Then paste your menu on a piece of wood or bark. Hang it by your door. Perhaps your imaginary friend will appear for lunch!

Make Your Very Own "Good Stuff" Box!

Find a sturdy box to hold all the "good stuff" you'll need to make and do all kinds of fun things. Decorate your box to suit your fancy, and begin to look for goodies to put in it.

You will need things like:

crayons	paste	tissue paper
markers	ribbon	pipe cleaners
tissues	buttons	fabric scraps
pencils	yarn	popsicle sticks
lace	beads	used greeting cards
bric-a-brac	scissors	AND. . . . .

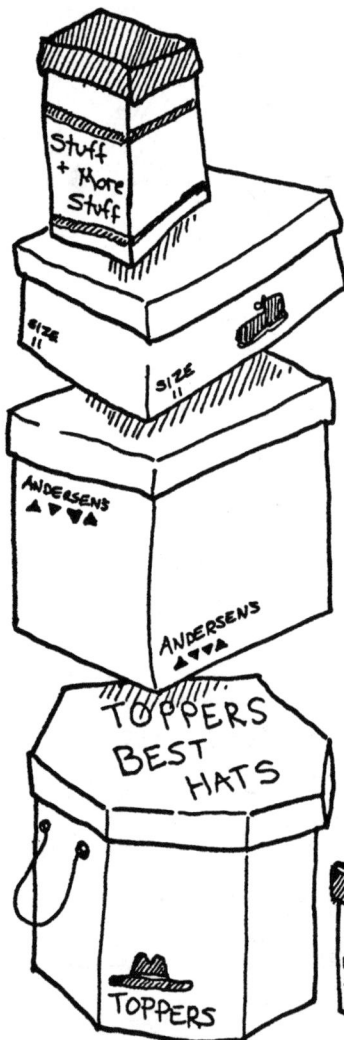

FAC...
T...

X-tra
Soft

FACIAL TISSUES

49¢

ASTE

. . . a whistle to blow
when you need
a grownup's help!

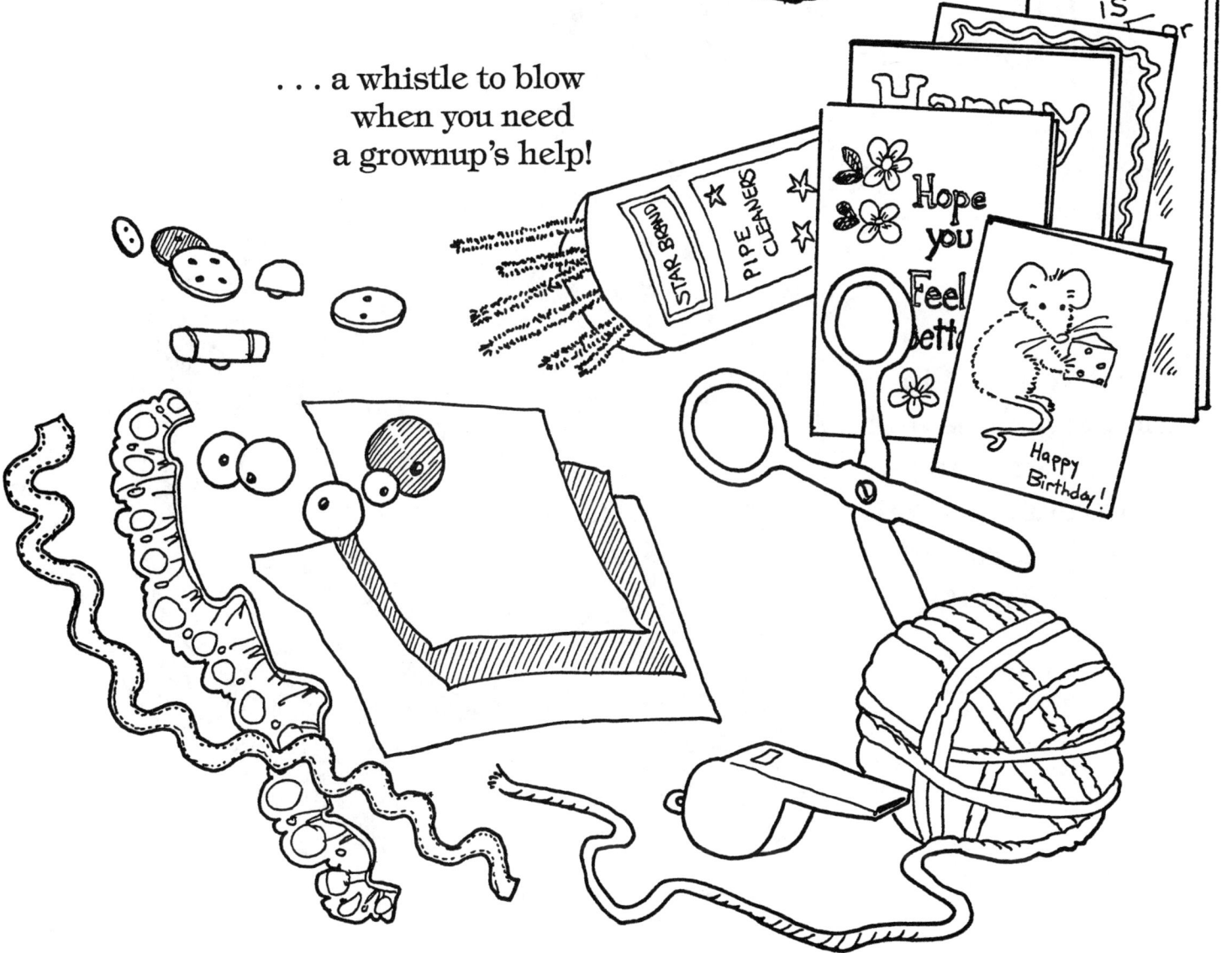

STAR BRAND
PIPE CLEANERS

This is for

Happy

Hope
you
Feel
Better

Happy
Birthday!

Put Yourself In The Driver's Seat

Put yourself in
the driver's seat of
a big jet plane,
a truck, a car,
a ship, a rocket,
or a train.

Make your instrument panel of old spools, buttons, metal and plastic lids, and shapes cut from cardboard. Maybe you can find an old watch or clock and a mirror or reflector to glue on, too. Find something round to use for a wheel.

Gallery Gallant

This gallery shows some silly pictures that are similar to some very famous real works of art.

Look at the sculpture and paintings very carefully.

Think of one or two words you might use to describe each one. The words can be serious or silly. Ask someone to help you write your words under each picture.

My Name Is _____

Color the pictures. Then show them to a grownup who might
be able to tell you the name of the real art represented by
by each one and the name of the artist who created it.

My Name Is _____

Kitchen Menagerie

Did you know that some very strange and silly animals hide away in kitchens?

If you look in a refrigerator, a vegetable box, the pantry, or cabinets for fruits, vegetables, eggs, and who knows what else, you might find some foods that can become unusual animals.

Create your very own animal menagerie by using junk from your "good stuff" box to turn food into wild and crazy creatures!

Just Imagine. . .

Lie down. Close your eyes. Pretend you are tucked into
bed on a very dark and stormy night. You are almost asleep.
Then the strangest things begin to happen.
Show with your body how you would react to each one.

The closet door opens slowly and . . .

you hear a munching sound.

A mouse jumps down on you.

A claw reaches out!

You hear a soft, purring sound.

Hurry . . . run back to bed! Cover up your head!

Tell Me A Story

Just suppose . . .
you fall asleep—then wake up
to find something on your head!

A furry hat

A jeweled crown

A helmet

A wizard's hat

A Native American headdress

Who are you?
Tell a story about yourself.

What If . . .

What if you stepped into a huge hole and fell
through a tunnel into a strange new world?
Can you imagine a story about meeting . . .

. . . a princess who is crying?

. . . a hairy monster?

a pickle with prickles?

. . . an upside-down donkey?

Make A "Love Note Tube" For Someone Special

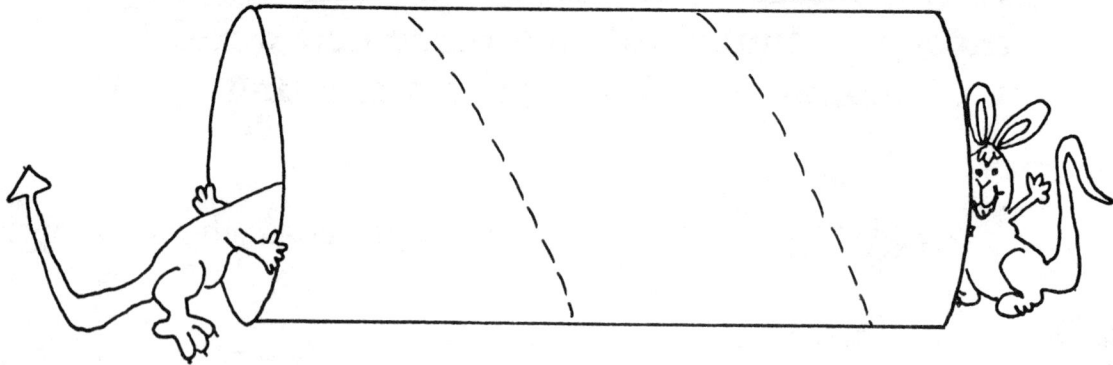

Cut tissue paper to cover
an empty toilet tissue roll.
(Leave some extra paper
on each end.)

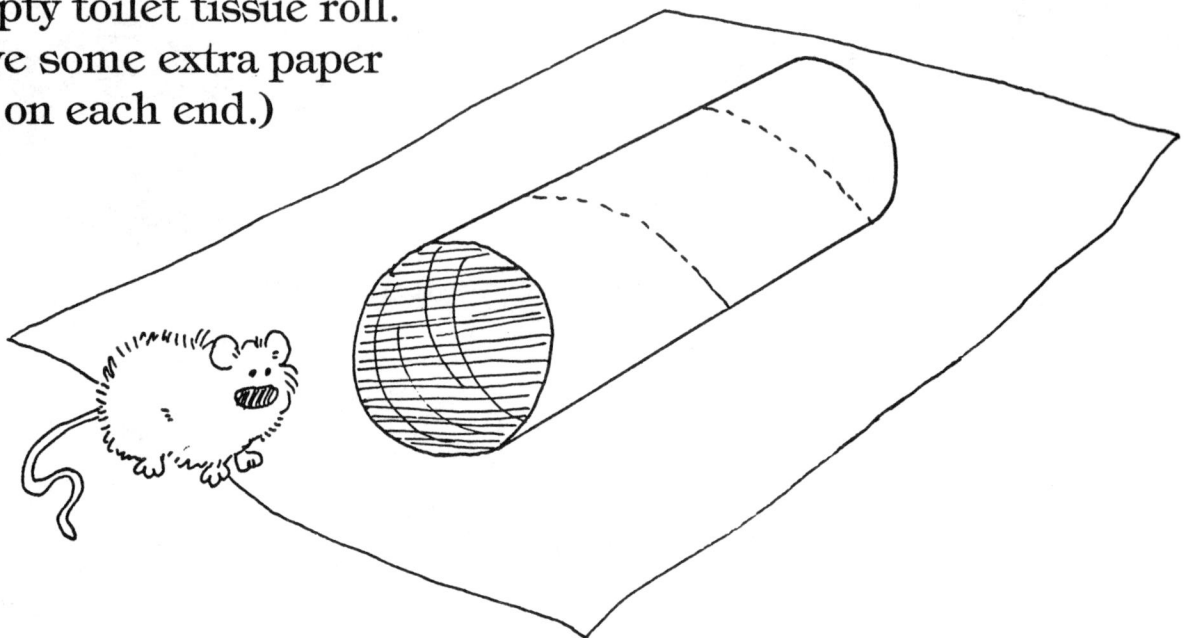

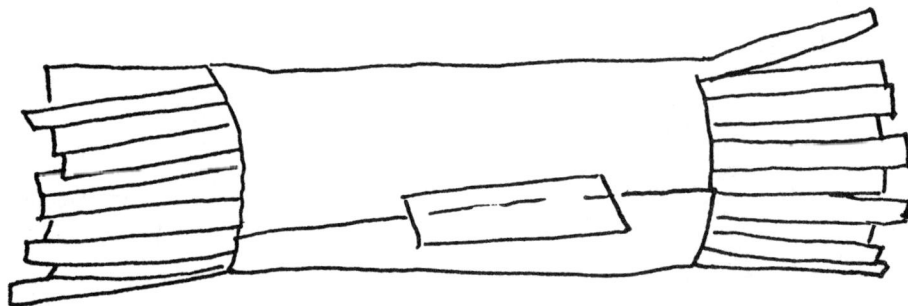

Paste the paper around the roll.
Fringe the ends.

Write a note to someone special
and scoot it inside the tube.

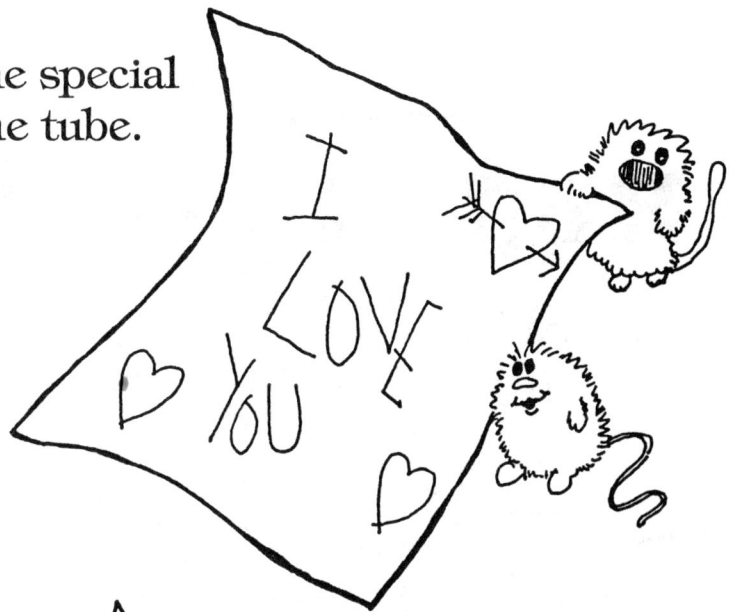

Tie the fringed ends
with ribbon or yarn.

Give the love note
tube and a big kiss to
your special person.

P.S. You might tuck a surprise inside the roll, such as a
picture you have made or a piece of gum or candy!

Faraway Places, Right Here At Home

You and your friends can use plain, ordinary objects
to create special hiding places like these.

Pretend it's a hunting camp, a secret cave,
a castle, a fort, a pirate ship, a ranger station,
or anything you want it to be.

Or it might be just a quiet place to read
or dream or think about important ideas!

SECRET HIDE OUT

It might be a place where you
can share secrets with a friend. *Shhh!*

You Don't Have To Paint With A Brush!

Paint the way Oliver Ostrich paints.

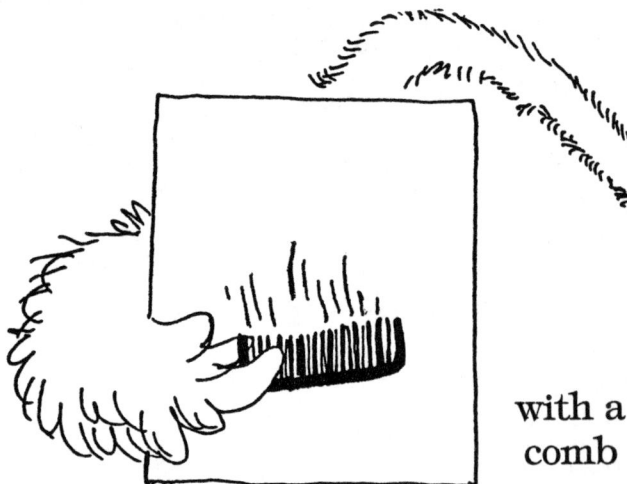

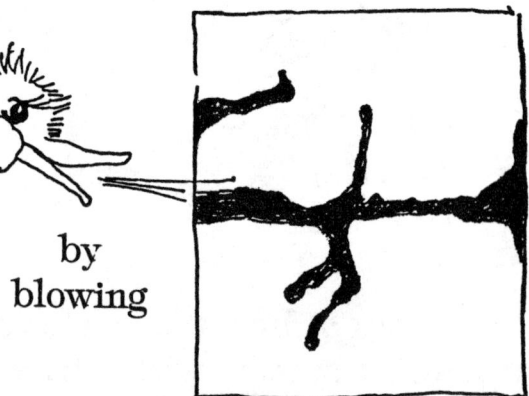

with a
feather

with a
stick

by
dripping

with a
fork

with a
comb

by
blowing

with a sponge

with a string

with a finger

with a leaf

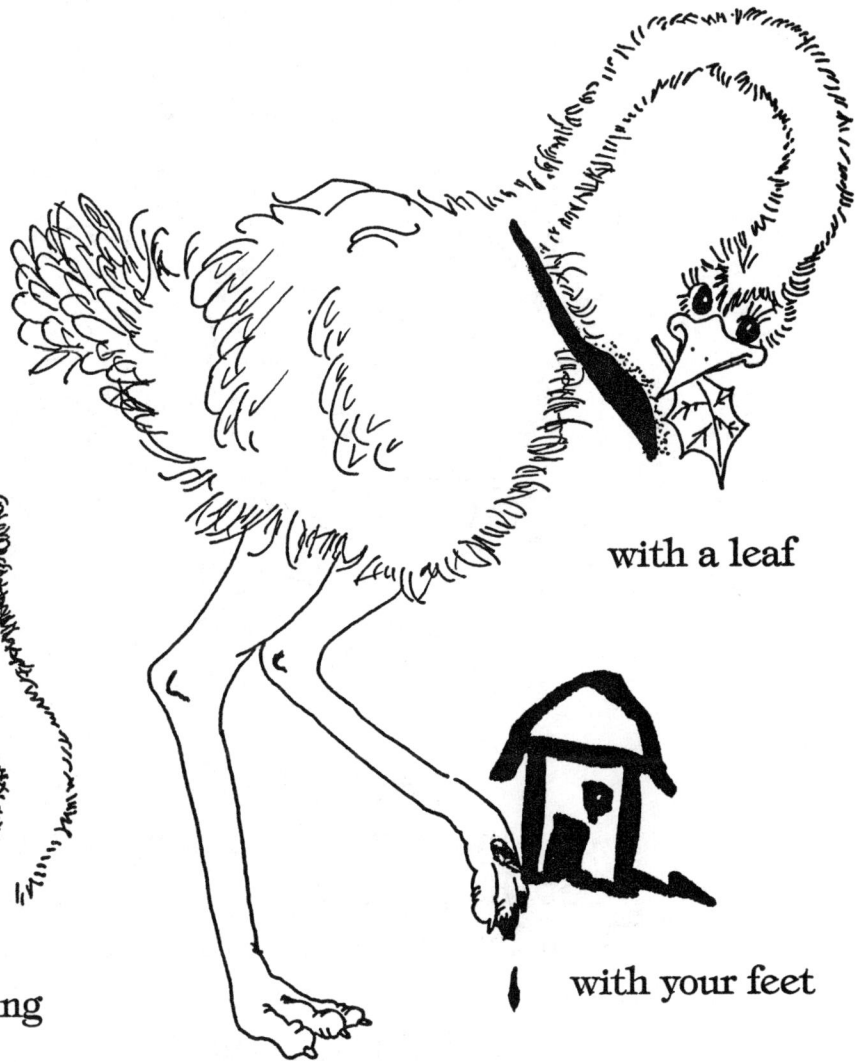

by squeezing

with your feet

You will need paint, paper, and some tools like Oliver's
to create your own pictures.

Some Rainy Day . . .

Sprinkle some dry tempera paint
or some dry colored sugar on a piece of paper.
Set the paper out in the rain for a few minutes.
Then bring it in to dry. You'll have a rain painting!

Lay your rain painting on the floor. Walk around it slowly
and look at it from all sides. How many different
objects or pictures can you imagine in the painting?

Alakazam!

Alakazam! Alakazee!
Color the spaces numbered 1, 2, and 3.
And when you do, you will find
A surprise of the most unusual kind!

My Name Is _____

How Many Ways Can You Think Of To Frame Your Artwork?

You could glue shells, pebbles, acorns, or cereal on cut cardboard.

You could paste it on colored paper.

You could paste it inside a box top.

For something very special, you could cover cardboard with velvet or silk. How about using wrapping paper or colored foil?

Play The Squiggle Game!

Ask someone to make a squiggle:
a curly line, a bumpy line,
any kind of shape or size.

Try to make a picture from this squiggle.

Like this!

Can you make some funny animals
beginning with these squiggles?

My Name Is _____

© 1995 by Incentive Publications, Inc., Nashville, TN.

Story Masks

Color each mask. Paste it on cardboard or heavy construction paper. Cut it out.

Add a handle to each one.

Use the masks to tell stories or perform plays, by yourself or with friends.

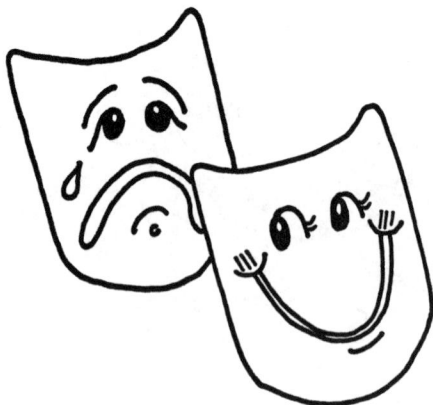

36 © 1995 by Incentive Publications, Inc., Nashville, TN.

Puppets, Puppets, Puppets!

Choose a puppet to make—it's easy!
Then you'll have someone to talk to!

(Your "good stuff" box will come in handy!)

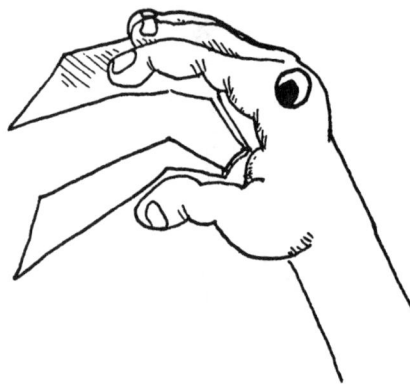

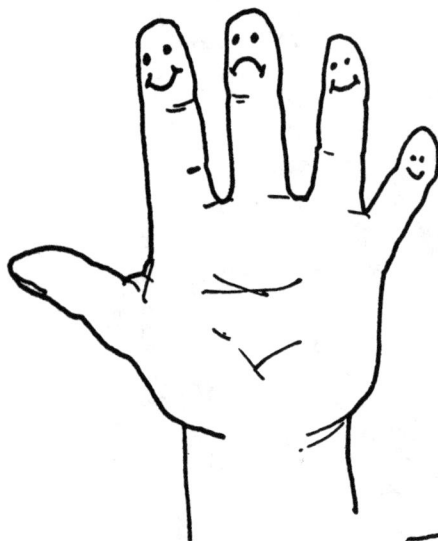

Make several puppets and put on a puppet show.
Use some of the ideas you see on these pages.

Paper Bag Puppets

Lunch-bag-size puppets are fun
and easy to create.

Draw the puppet face on the bottom of the bag.

Top of mouth goes here.

Bottom of mouth goes here.

Look at these models and use the patterns
on the next page to make your puppets.
Add string and yarn or pieces of colored paper and fabric
scraps to add your own special touch to each puppet.

Sing Up—Sing Down!

You can make your voice step up and down
just as if it were a stairway.
These steps will help you sing a song.
Ask someone to sing with you.
Point to each step with your finger as you sing.

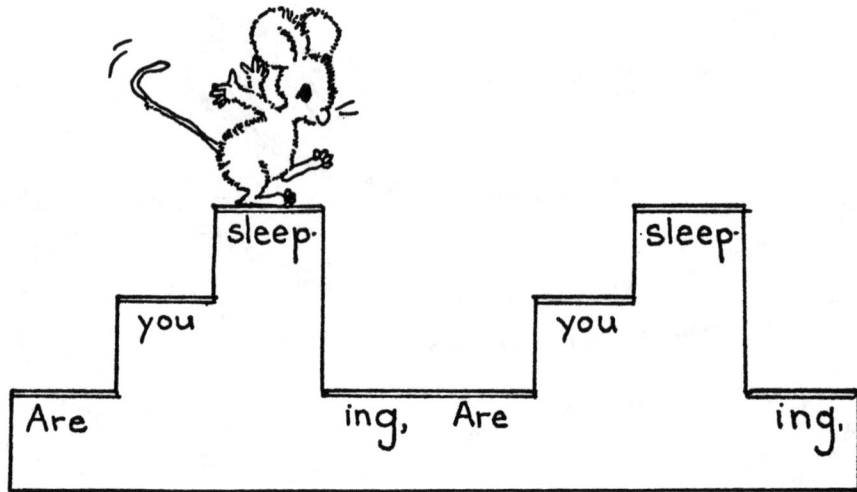

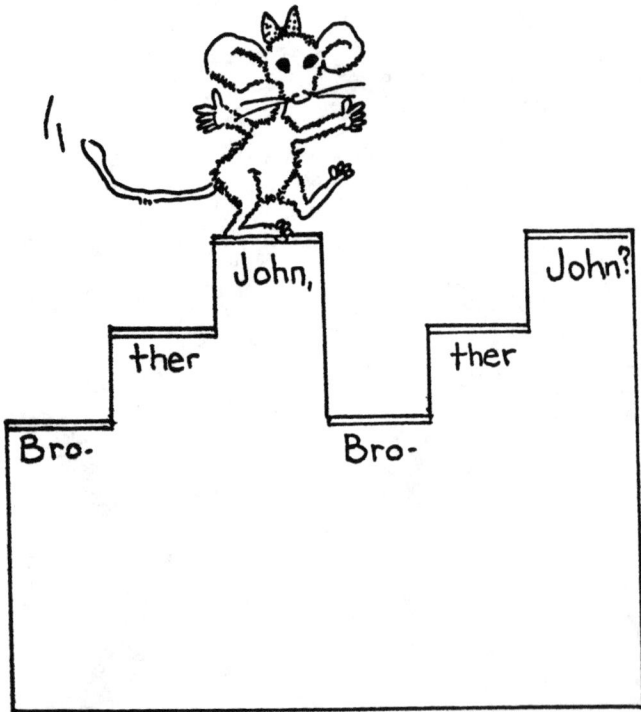

sleep·   sleep·
you   you
Are   ing,   Are   ing,

John,   John?
ther   ther
Bro·   Bro·

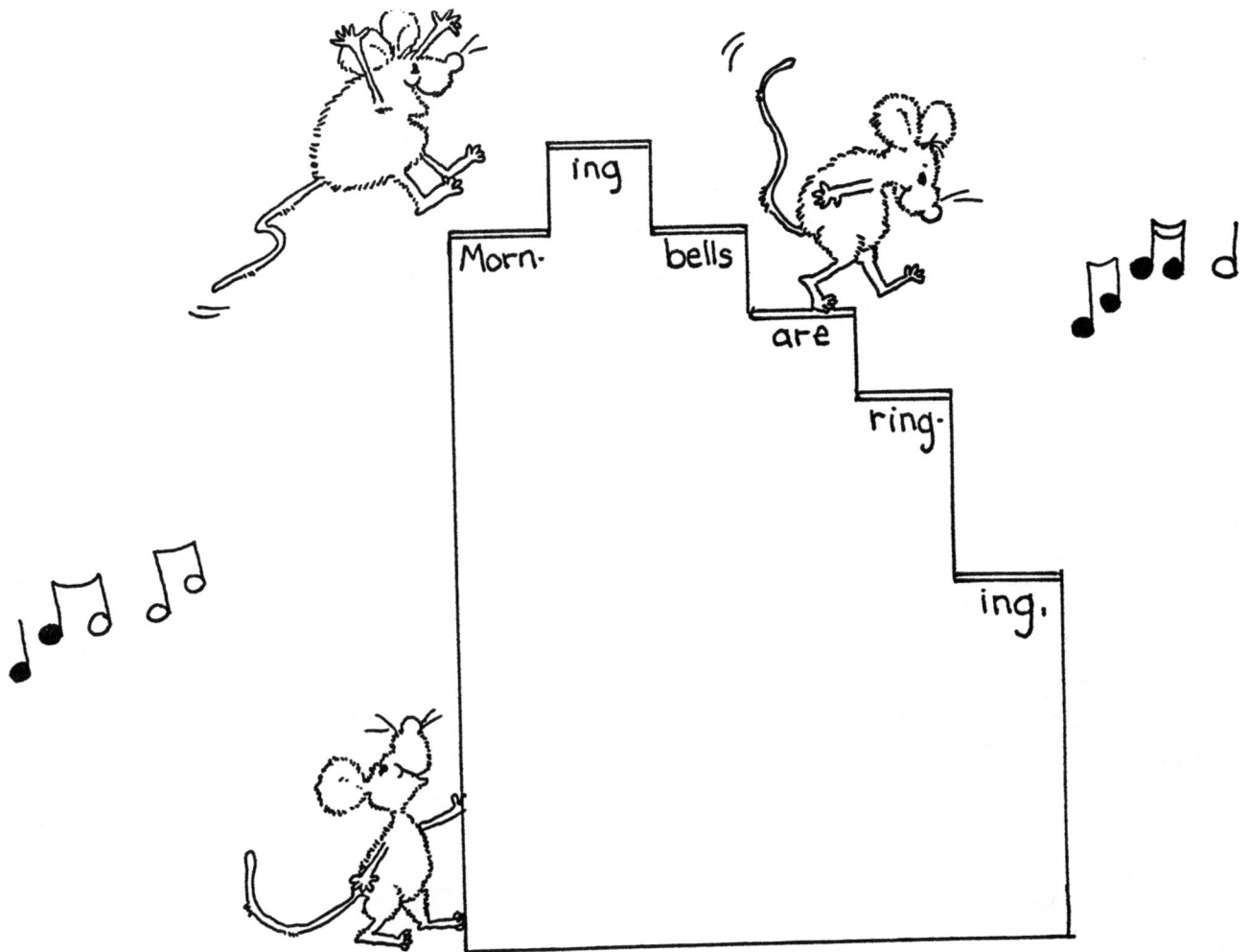

High And Low

You can sing a picture!
Follow the lines with your voice.

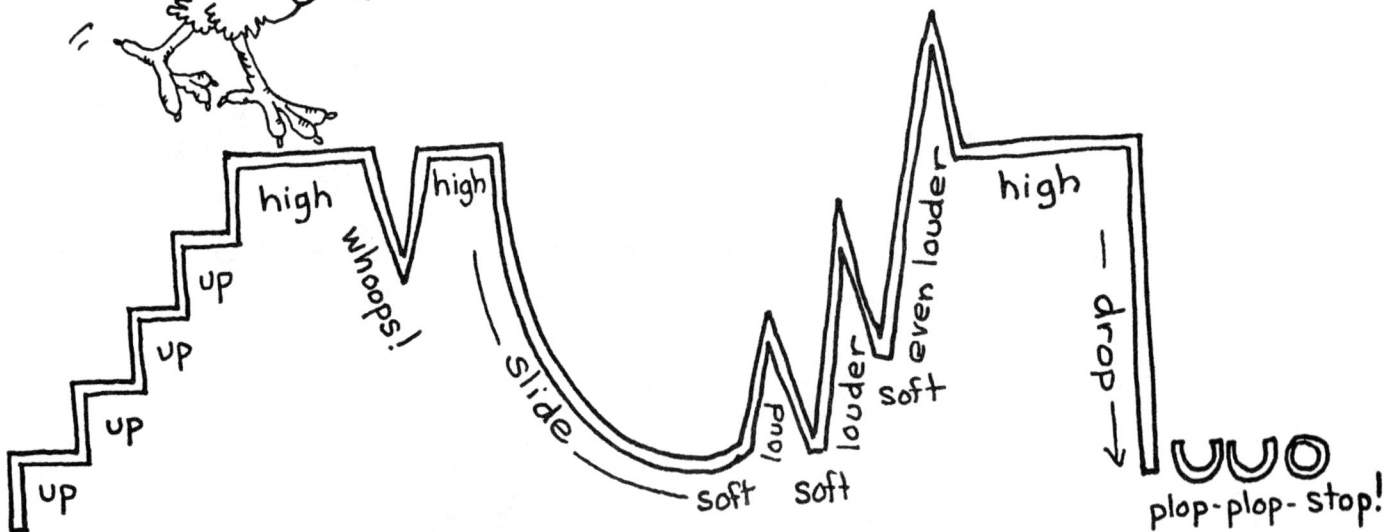

Trace with your finger as you sing a ride on the roller coaster. Make your voice go high and low, loud and soft

up
up
up
up
high
whoops!
high
slide
soft
soft
loud
louder
even louder
soft
high
— drop →
plop-plop-stop!

Sing the adventure of the Kangarooster!

What Can You Do With A Box?

Find a box you like.
Select crayons, paste, paper, and lots
of goodies from your "good stuff" collection
to make your box into something interesting.

You could make a house, a train,
a treasure chest, a home for an animal,
or who knows what else . . .

Have a "boxing bee" with your friends or classmates. Set up a
workshop in which everyone creates his or her own box thing.
Then have a "box show" to share and tell about your boxes!

Silly Story . . .

Would you like to come to a birthday party for my pet mouse, Wilbur? Well, first you will have to drink shrinking potion so you will be small enough to fit into Wilbur's mouse house. Can you imagine what we will eat, and what Wilbur's gifts will be...

Have you ever been to an upside-down birthday party? Well, let me tell you about the one I went to!

Ask someone to read these silly story starters.
Choose one or two stories to finish.
Maybe your reader will help you write your story in the blank spaces.

My Name Is _____

. . . . Starters

Once upon a time there was a very tall boy who got a very tall present for his birthday. From inside the present was coming a very loud noise....

Once there was a funny little girl who gave herself a huge birthday party to which she invited only witches, goblins, fairies and giants. What strange guests arrived at her door.... and what strange gifts they brought....

Use the long spaces at the bottom of each page
to illustrate your stories.

My Name Is _____

The Whole World's A Stage

... and you are an actor or actress!

You can create special places to give
plays by cutting and pasting and
pinning and painting things like these.

Use your own wonderful ideas and
ask some friends to work with you!

Be Somebody!

Put on a costume and have some fun,
Pretend you are something or even someone!
A pirate, a flower, a clown, or a queen,
A cowboy, a doctor, or any object you've seen . . .

A puppet, an octopus, a robot, a dragon,
Or a donkey that pulls a fancy pink wagon,
A fairy, a witch, or a prince with a ring—
In a make-believe world you can be anything!

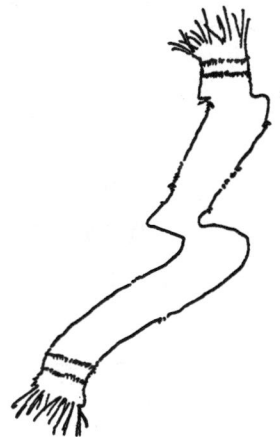

BONZO SOAP

Choose someone or something you'd like to be.
The pictures will give you some ideas for costumes.

Do The "String Thing"

Get a big ball of string and try to think of
some unusual things to do with it.

Tie a package.

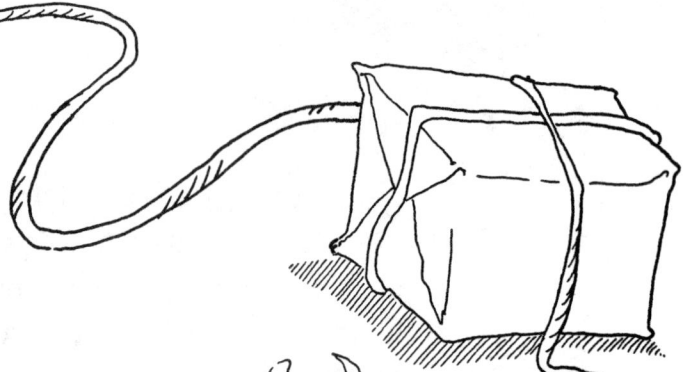

Put it on the floor and walk on it.

Use it to write your name.

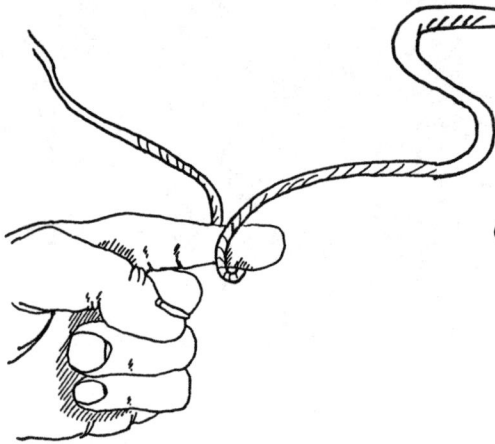

Tie it around your finger or your waist.
Weave it in and out through your fingers
or your buttonholes or the eyes of your shoes.

OR . . . Break off a nice long piece.
Dip it in paint, and pull it across
a piece of drawing paper to make
your very own "string thing" picture.

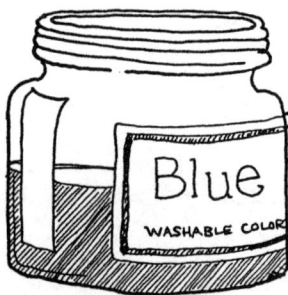

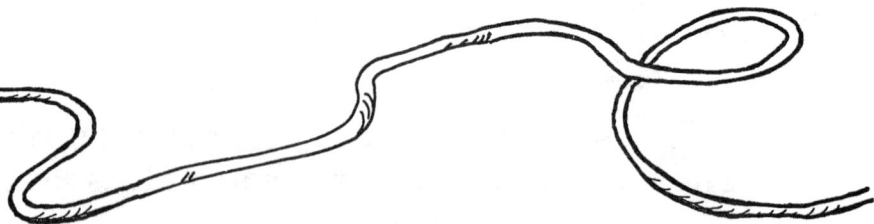

Blue
WASHABLE COLOR

Can You Do The Crocodile Crunch?

Corky Crocodile has a creak in his tail.
Every time he moves, it squeaks.

Creak Creak!

Use the patterns on the next two pages
to make yourself a crocodile tail.
Pin or tie your tail on the back of your shirt or pants.

Pretend you are Corky at a dance.
Ask a friend to "accompany" you
by using his mouth or an instrument
to make the squeaky sounds for Corky while you move.

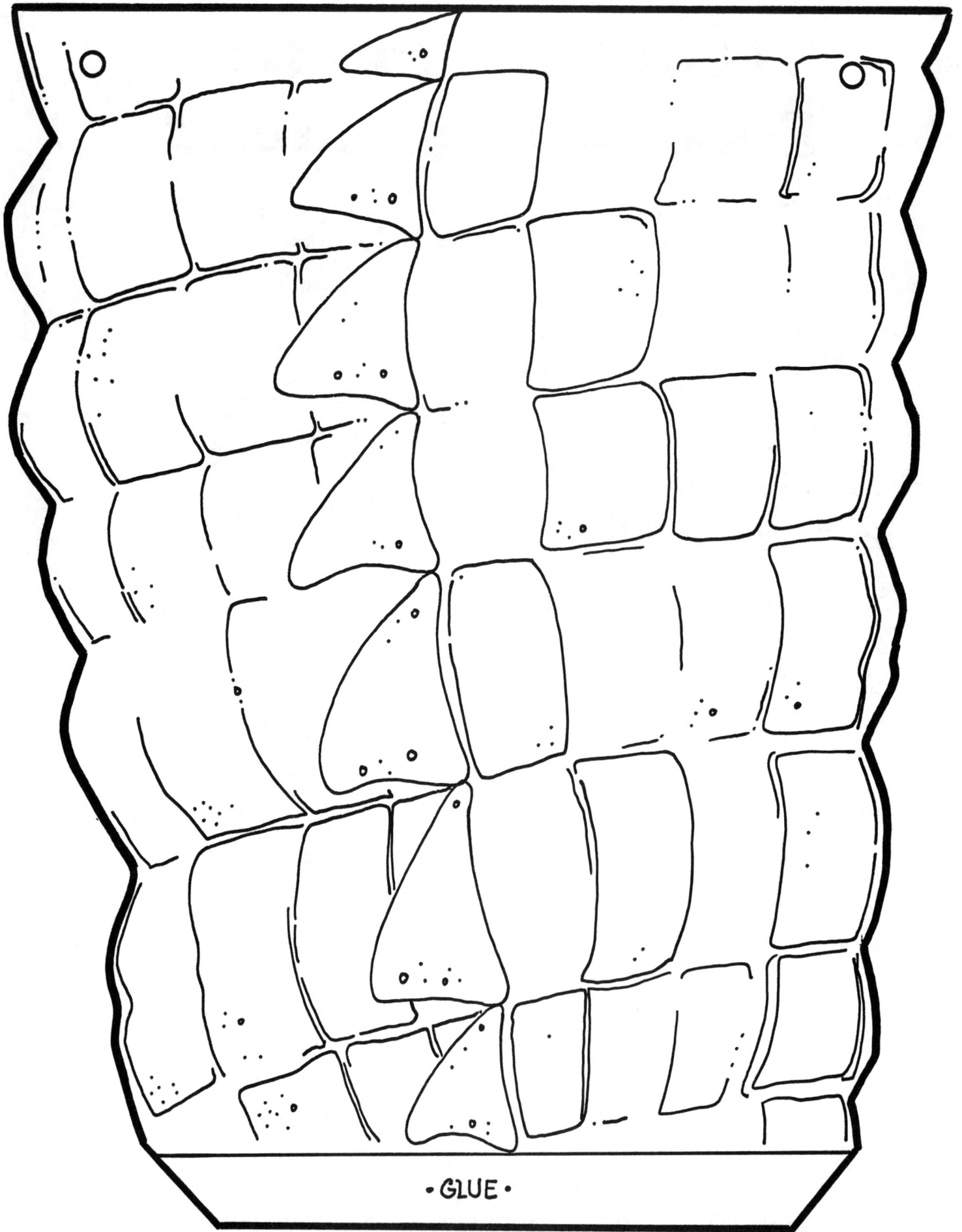

· GLUE ·

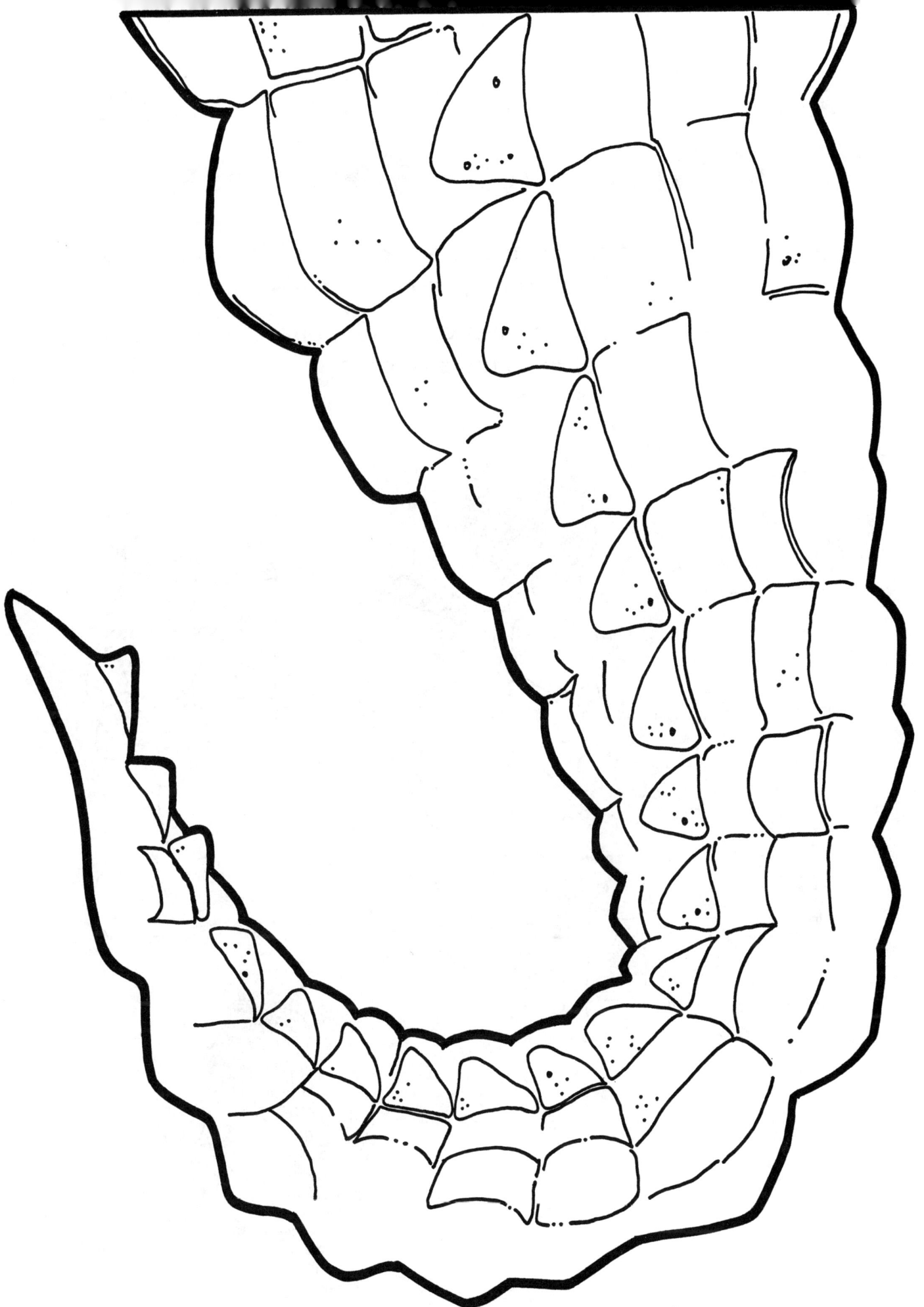

You May Have Rhythm Wherever You Go!

Look carefully at the pictures to see what kinds of things these children are using as rhythm instruments.

Ask someone to help you make one or two simple instruments.

Invite some friends to join you
for marching or skipping or dancing.

OR . . . Be a one-person band. See how many instruments
you can play at the same time. You might choose a
favorite cassette tape as your accompaniment.

Cut A Paper Caper!

Fold a long piece of paper
in four or more equal sections.

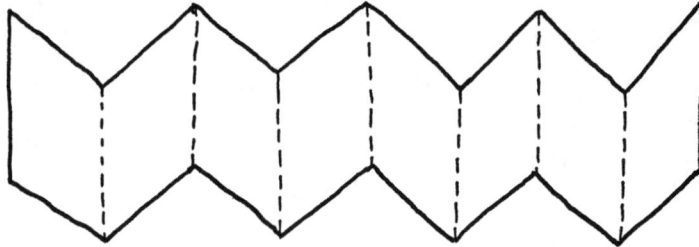

On the top section, draw a design
or picture that touches the fold on
both sides in at least one place.

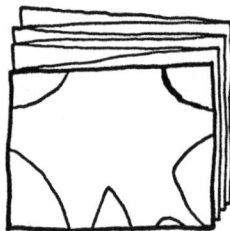

Cut out the design, but be careful not
to cut away the folded edges at the
places where the picture touches.

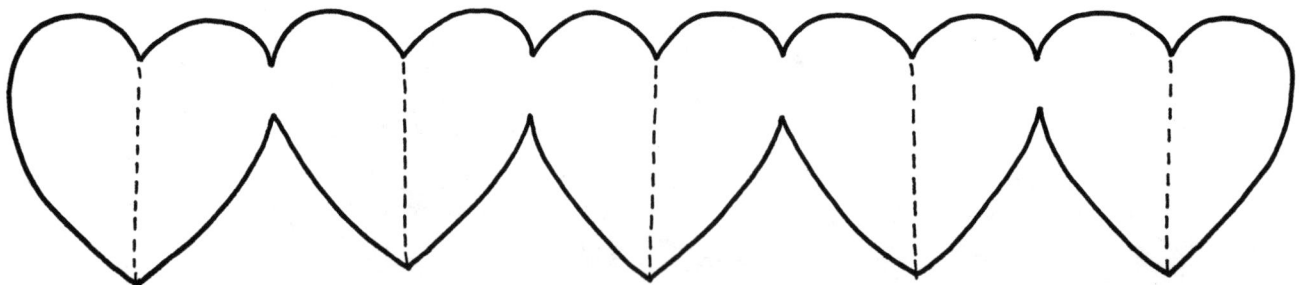

A Squiggle Card Is Fun To Make!

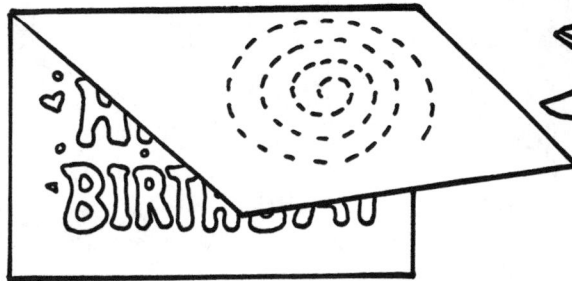

Make a card that folds like this.
Write your message on the bottom half ONLY.

Make a hole with your scissors in the
center of the top. Then cut around and
around to make a long, snake-like squiggle.

Paste the top card to the bottom card
at the edges and corners ONLY.

Attach a pretty piece of yarn or ribbon
to the end of the squiggle.

The message appears when the receiver pulls on the ribbon!

"Y" Is For You

Ask someone to help you cut the first letter of your name
from a very large piece of paper.
Make it as large as the paper allows.
Paint it.
Paste it on another large, flat piece of plain paper.
Decorate your initial by gluing lots of different things on it.
Use objects from your "good stuff" box, or collect
materials such as buttons, scraps of cloth and colored
paper, beans, string, and cereal.
Hang your initial in a very important place.

60

"Eye" Can See It!

How good is your artist's eye?
Some objects and animals are hidden in this picture.
Can you find . . .

. . . an elephant, a pipe, a lollipop, a top hat, at least two

triangles, two ants, a fish, a toothbrush, a chicken leg,

a comb, three raindrops, and the numerals 9, 3 and 8?

Circle each one as you find it.

My Name Is _____

Lights Out!

Use a piece of black construction paper
and yellow crayon or chalk to create a
"dark night" picture.

(If you use fluorescent paint,
your picture will glow in the dark.)

Designer's Safari

Pretend you are on a jungle safari.
Find the hidden animals by following the
directions to color the design below.

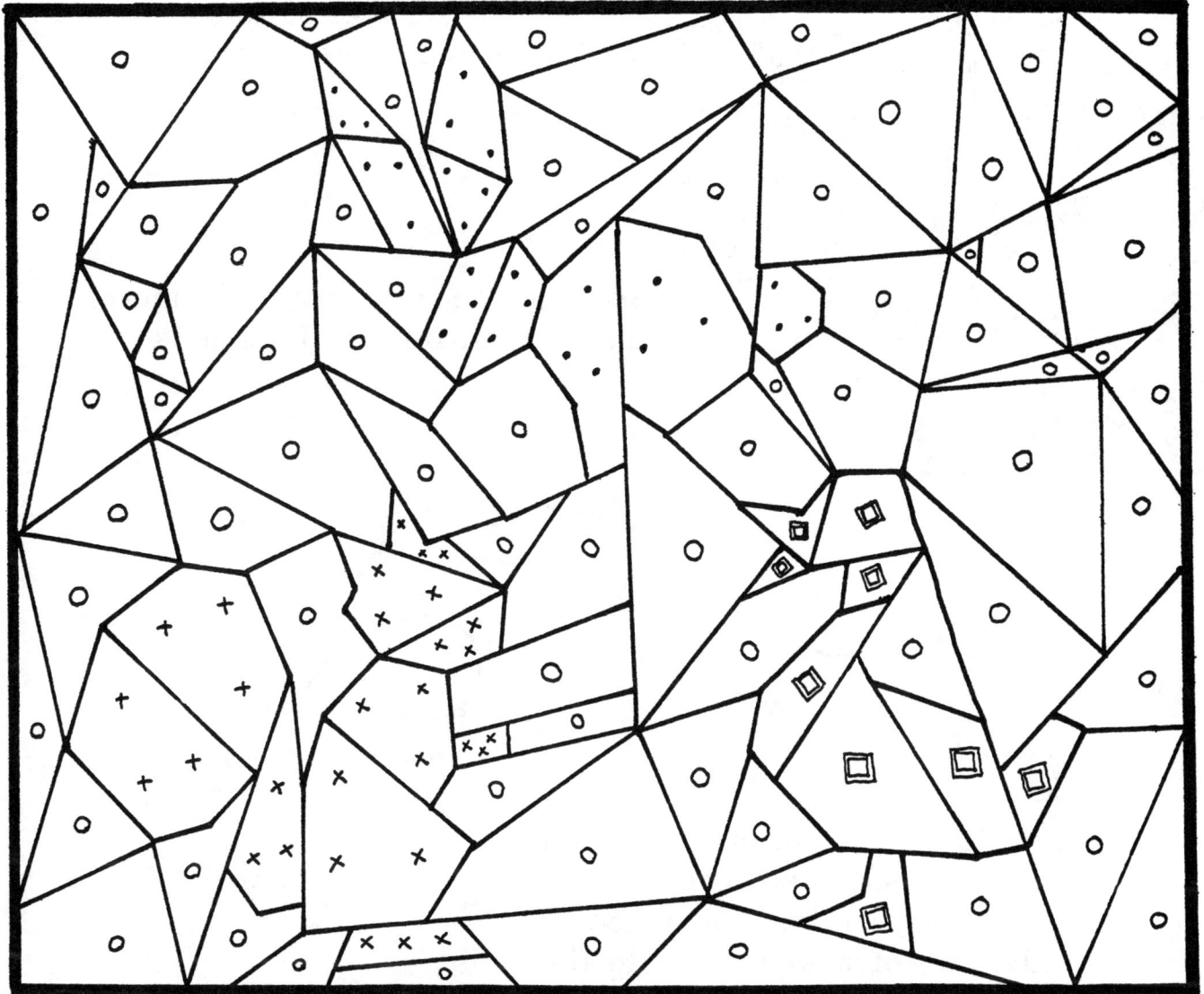

Color all spaces with O green.

Color all spaces with X red.

Color all spaces with ▫ yellow.

Color all spaces with · · · brown.

My Name Is _____

63

Shape A Dough-Re-Mi Doodle Dandy!

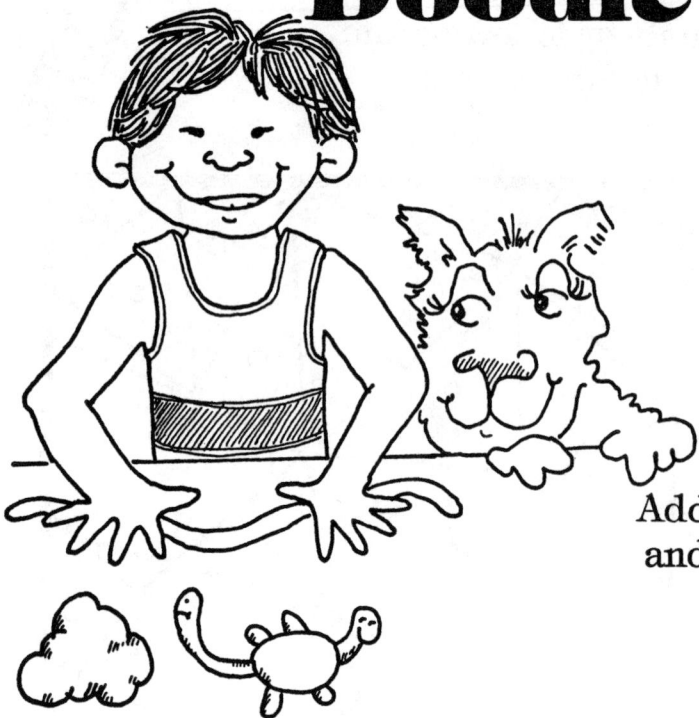

Mix together with your hands:
2 cups of salt
2 cups of flour
½ cup of shortening

Add slowly ½ cup of water (or more) and keep mixing until dough is not too sticky.

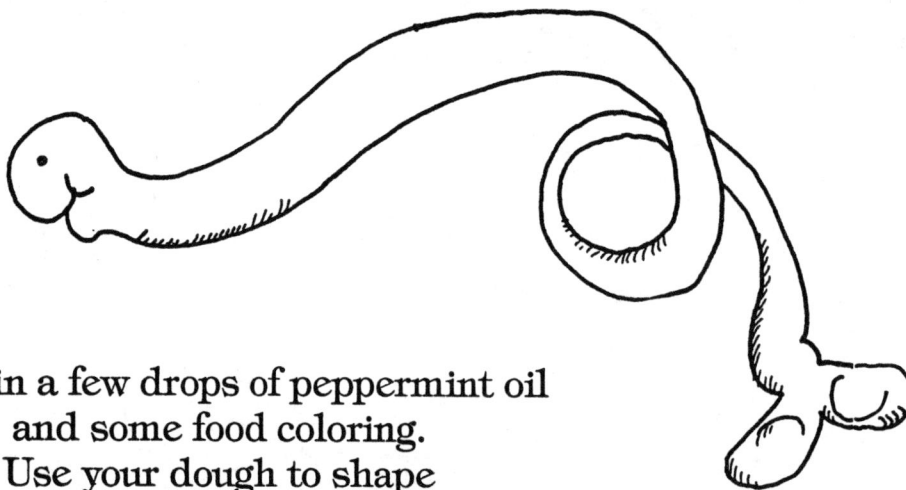

Work in a few drops of peppermint oil and some food coloring.
Use your dough to shape all kinds of make-believe doodles.

Party Popper

Color the faces on the Party Popper. Then cut along the dotted lines.
Look at the directions on page 66 to see how to fold it.

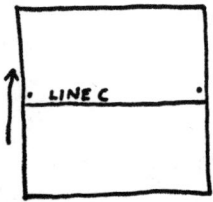

① fold forewards along LINE C and open.

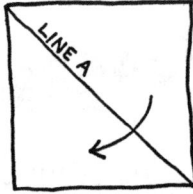

② fold back along LINE A and open.

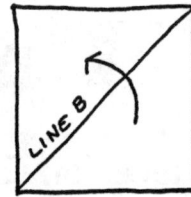

③ fold back along LINE B and open.

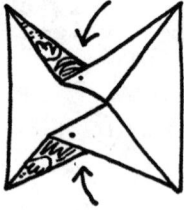

④ push in on line C.

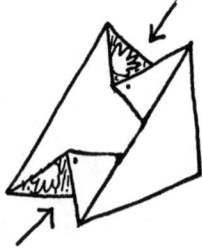

⑤ push together into a triangle.

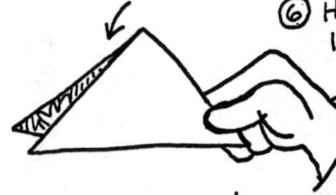

⑥ Hold the popper like this. Raise your arm and bring the Party Popper down with a fast snapping motion. BANG!

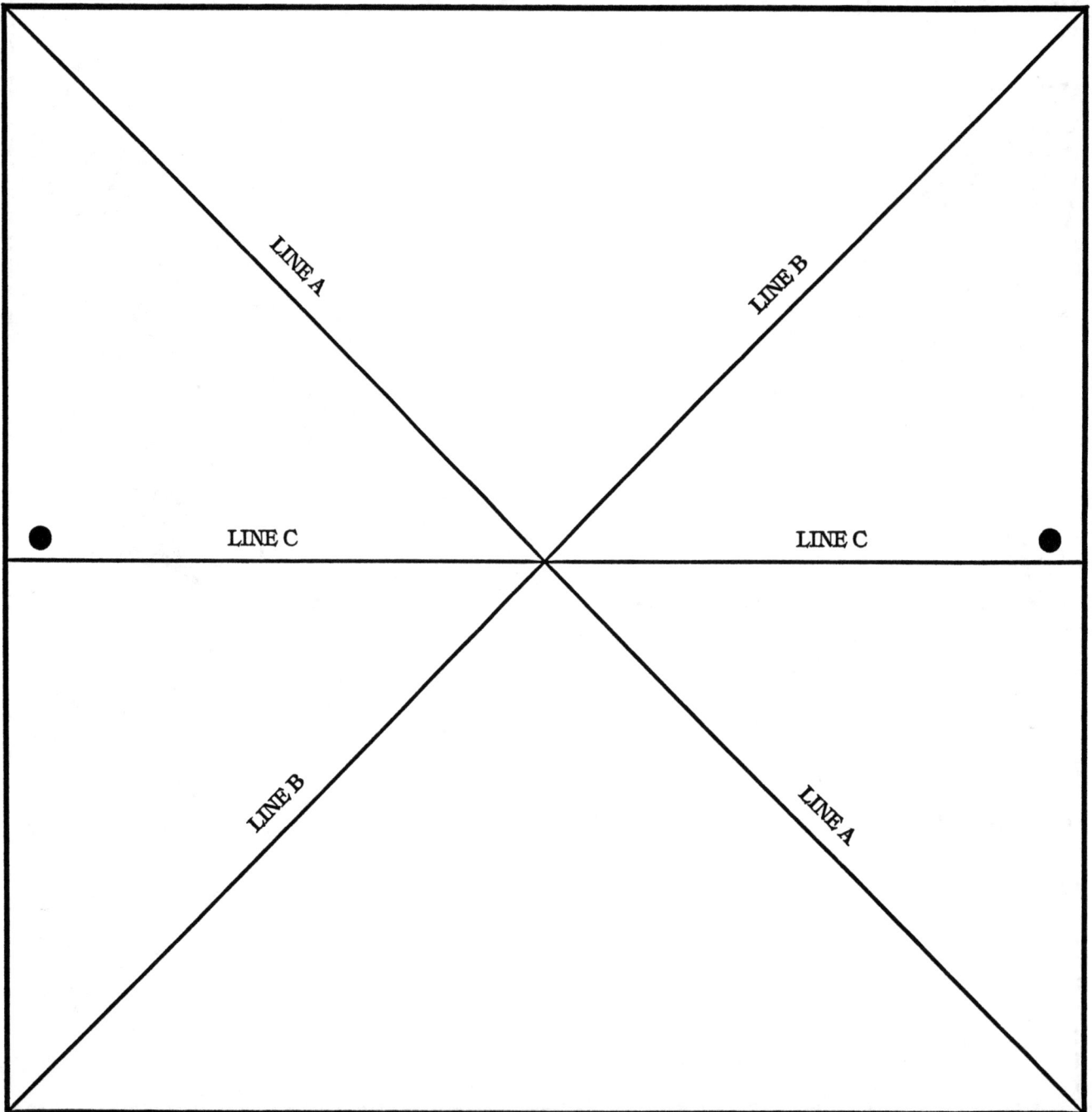

LINE C

LINE A

LINE B

LINE A

LINE B

LINE C

LINE C

LINE B

LINE A

Could-Be, Can't-Be Beasts

Color the animal pictures on the next five pages.
Then cut them apart carefully on the dotted lines.

You will have all the pieces you need to create
some crazy, mixed-up, wonderful new animals.

Use the pieces like a puzzle
to put together several new
"could-be but can't-be" animal creations.
Paste your new animals on a big sheet of
paper to hang on the wall in your room.
Give each new animal a name!

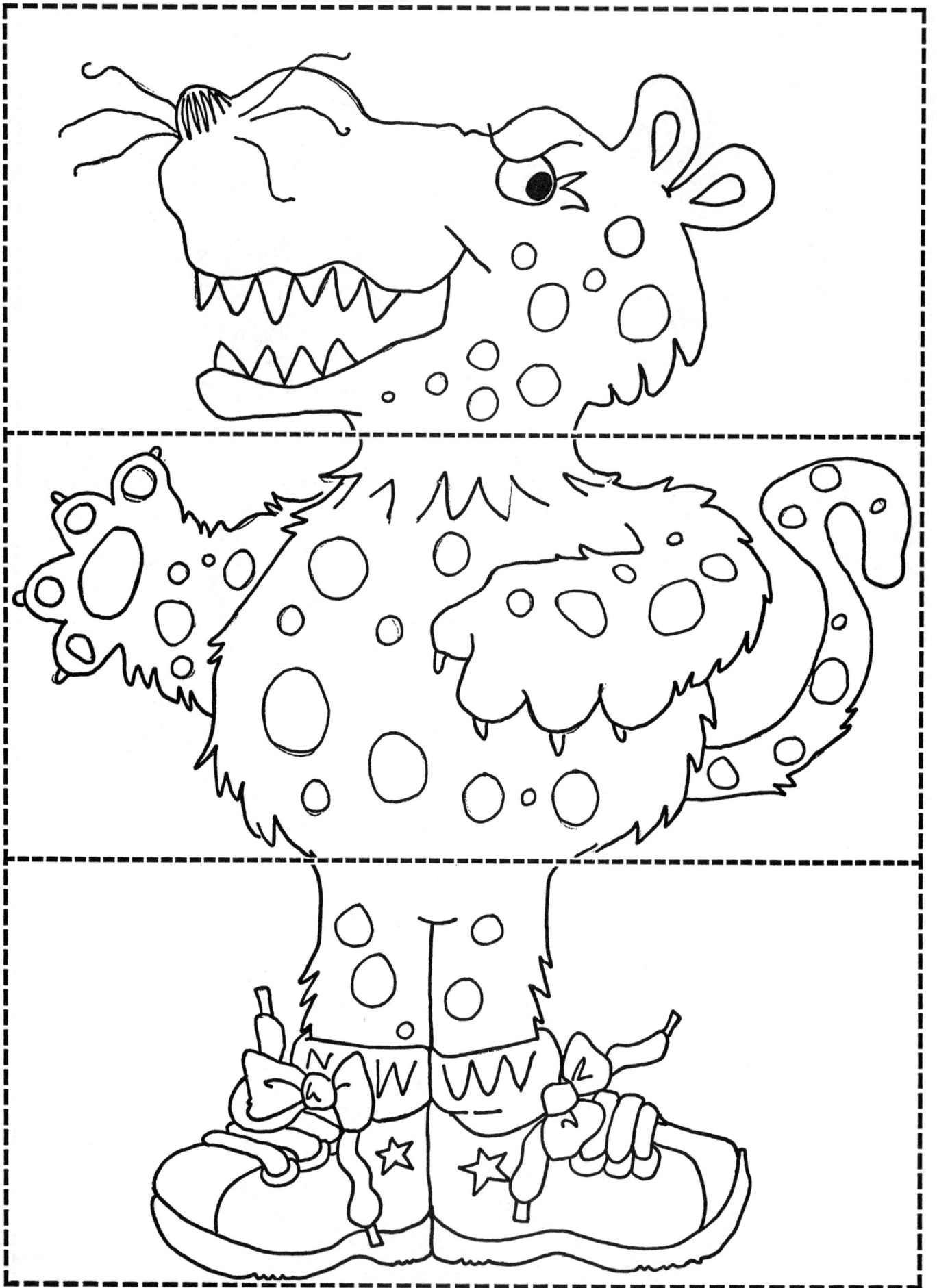

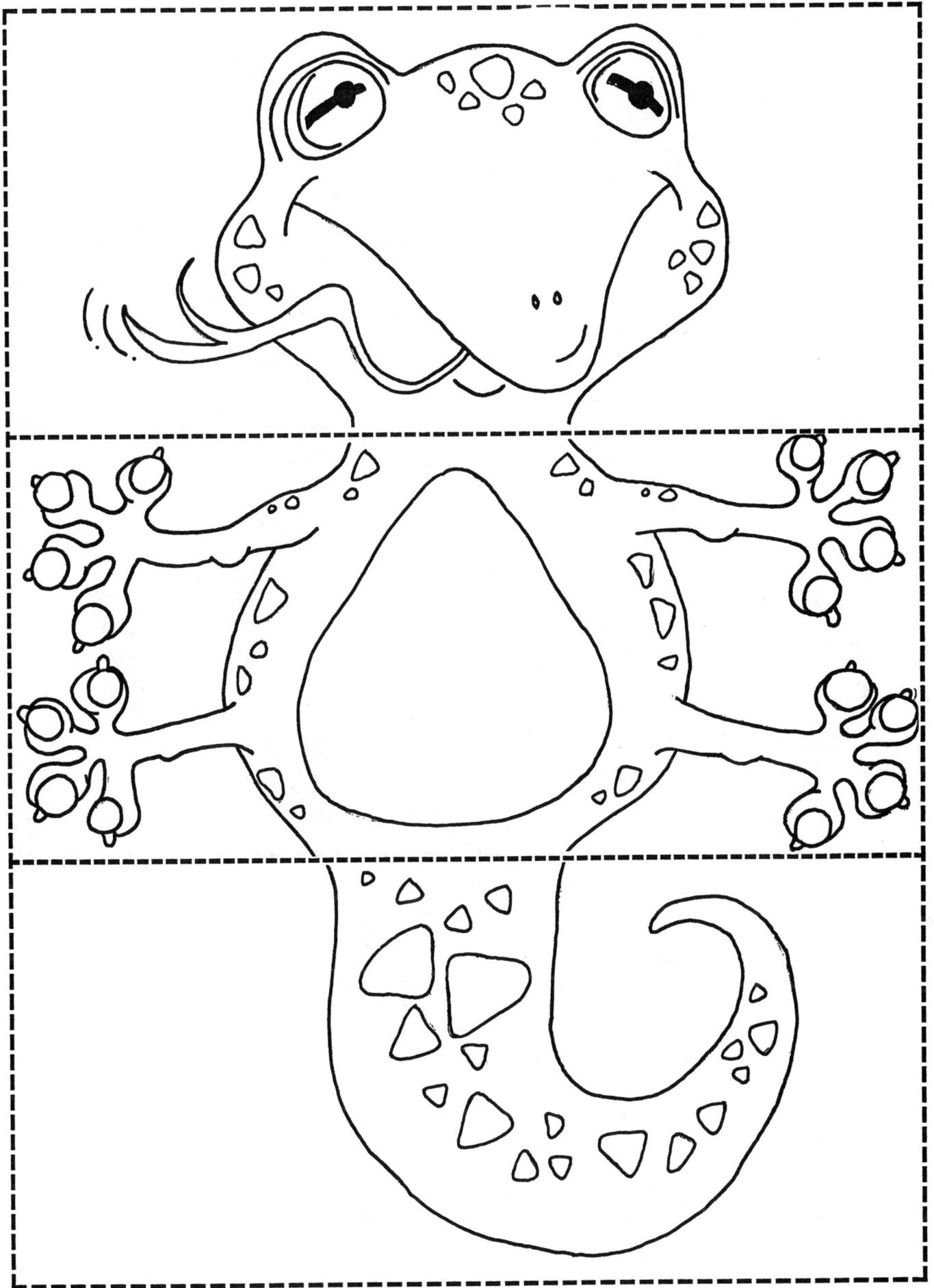

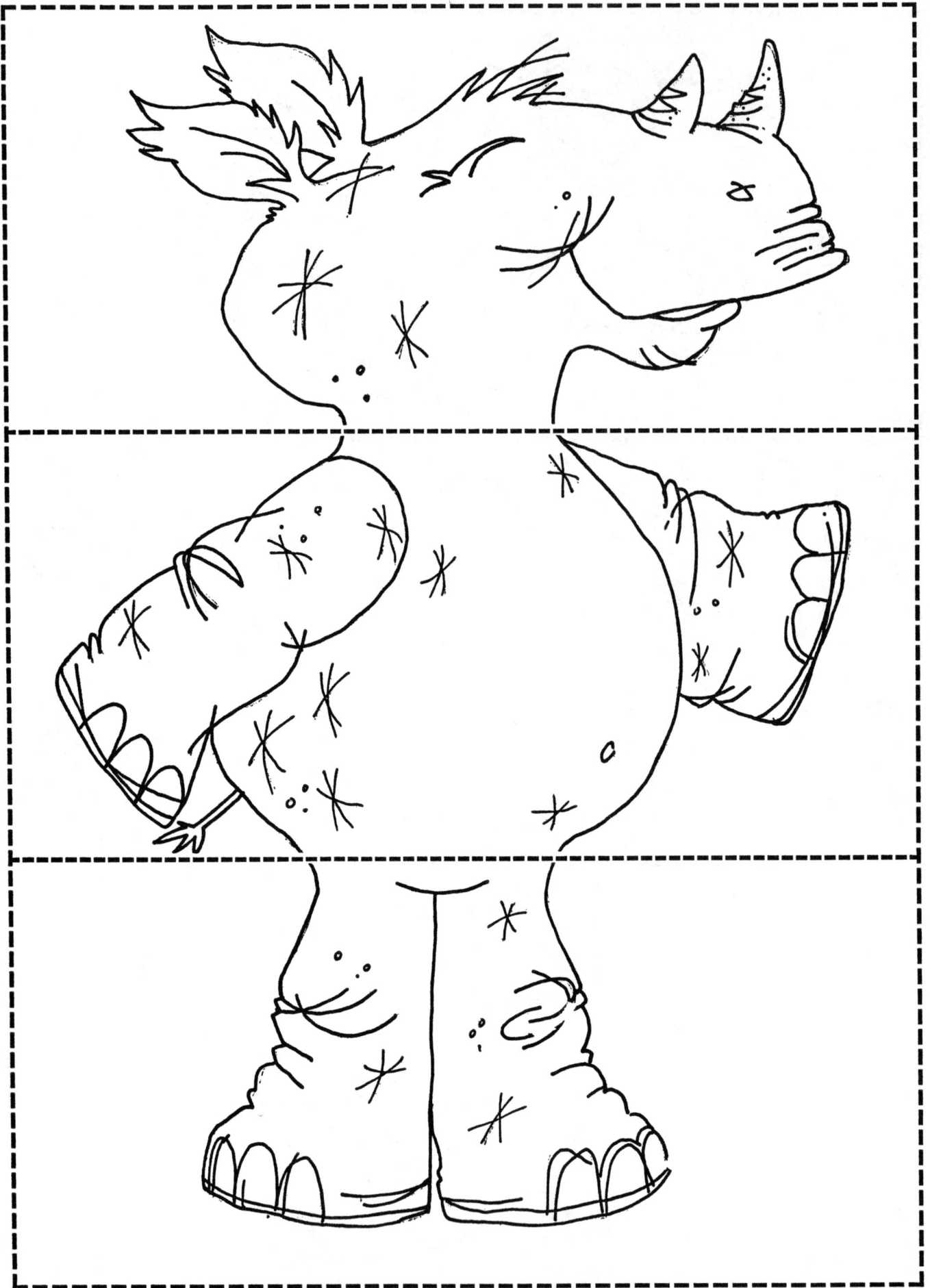

72

Wind Your Way Through This Zany Zoo

EXIT

ENTRANCE

. . . but don't let a thing get a bite of YOU!

My Name Is _____

Everybody Needs . . .
A Special Thinking Place

Find a quiet spot where you can think a poem, sing a song, or dream a dream.
Draw your thought or dream
in the special "thinking" place in the picture.

My Name Is _____

Act It Out

Make a stage for the classroom. Plan and present a play ("The Three Little Pigs," "Little Red Riding Hood," or "The Three Billy Goats Gruff").

Sing "Clap Your Hands" from *Fireside Book of Children's Songs*, collected and edited by Marie Winn (Simon and Schuster). Then make rhythm band instruments and stage a parade.

Make family members (or characters from favorite stories) on posterboard. Cut holes for faces and hands, and draw on facial features and body parts. Have fun acting out the characters.

Ask children to make up their own silly stories for other children to act out. For example:
> Wiggly Willy liked to act silly.
> Sometimes Wiggly Willy wiggled his toes.
> Sometimes Wiggly Willy wiggled his nose.
> Silly Wiggly Willy also liked to squiggle and squirm just like a fish.
> With his arms for two flippers, and his feet for a tail,
> Silly Wiggly Willy would pretend he's a whale!

Use paper plates as masks. Draw on the features, or glue on feathers and yarn, and add a tongue depressor to hold the mask. Use these masks to dramatize "Farmer in the Dell," "Old MacDonald Had a Farm," or another old favorite.

Provide a collection of hats (the more imaginative, the better) to encourage children to become many different characters.

Ask children to dream up special hiding places for tiny creatures of their imagination: a leprechaun, a magic mouse, a dwarf, a singing grasshopper, or a lily queen. Then have them act out the imaginary creatures in hiding.

Ten Terrific Things To Do With Tempera Paint . . .

1. Put tempera paint in roll-on deodorant bottles.
2. Roll toy cars through paint.
3. Fingerpaint with pudding or shaving cream instead of paint.
4. Paint with a cotton swab.
5. Put paper in the bottom of an aluminum foil roll pan. Put marbles in small foil bowls filled with different colors of paint. Swirl marbles in the paint, and then place them in the roll pan to create unique designs.
6. Use a brayer and roll on the paint.
7. Make a ring from a coat hanger and put a spool on it. Roll this around in the paint and then on the paper.
8. Just for fun, you might want to add sand, corn starch, sawdust, or detergent powder to tempera paint for a rough texture, or add some cinnamon or allspice for a scented picture.
9. Paint rainy day "swirl" pictures. Sprinkle several different colors of dry pastel-colored tempera paint on pieces of shelf paper or butcher paper. Place them outside in the rain for a brief time. Bring inside and gently shake from side to side to mix the colors. Place on newspapers and leave to dry.
10. Use wax crayons to draw nighttime sky scenes containing brightly colored moons and stars. Mix a dry black tempera paint with water to make a very thin wash. Use a paintbrush to completely cover the crayon picture with the black wash. Allow to dry. Use the same technique to cover gaily colored spring drawings of birds, bees, flowers, and trees with a light blue wash.

. . . And Two Unusual Ways To Use Chalk

1. Paint Buttermilk Chalk Pictures. Put a teaspoonful of buttermilk on damp fingerpaint paper. Direct child to use chalk through the milk.
2. Make chalk designs in a bottle.
    Use: • aluminum tart or pot pie tins
         • salt
         • colored chalk
         • white glue
         • small juice bottle with top or cork, or baby food jar with lid
    Do: • Select a piece of chalk.
         • Pour a little salt in the bottom of the tin. Rub the piece of chalk in the salt until the salt becomes colored to your liking.
         • Pour the colored salt into the bottom of the bottle. Tilt the jar or bottle slightly to make the colored design more interesting.
         • Choose a compatible color of chalk and make another layer. Use a pencil or toothpick to make a tunnel down along the side of the jar into the previous layer. The new color will fill in as the pencil is removed.
         • Continue making layers until the jar is filled.
         • Seal with glue after you have filled in the top layer.
         • Replace lid or cork.

Art Smart

One of the best ways to encourage young children to stretch their imaginations and to develop unique artistic abilities is to help them find ways to use ordinary materials in extraordinary ways. When a discarded bottle becomes a treasured vase for a wildflower bouquet, a brown paper lunch bag turns into a puppet pal, and old buttons on a string become a one-of-a-kind necklace, entirely new avenues for creative thinking are opened.

It is important to arrange the environment to create a positive and stress-free setting in which children are provided with opportunities to explore and experiment with a variety of materials and techniques without undue pressure or predetermined outcomes. Lots of old newspapers to cover work surfaces, easels or tables of a proper height and dimension to fit the children's developmental needs, large crayons, pencils, and paintbrushes, and "elbow room" for working are essential components of the creative corner. Adults' old shirts which have been altered by removing the sleeves make wonderful artist's smocks for budding artists when worn backwards.

Decorate a big, round hat box or a big basket with a handle to hold "good stuff" for group projects. You may also want to help each child make a personal "good stuff" container from a shoe box. (Shoe boxes are sturdy and stack easily for shelf storage.) Just for fun, use the "good stuff" immediately to make a multimedia collage or diorama.

At another time, try to find items in your "good stuff" collection to use to create three-dimensional items, such as a telephone, a typewriter, a cash register, a clock, or a radio. Use the completed instruments to spark on-the-spot creative dramatics.

As a wind-down activity following directed teaching sessions or outdoor play, make large outlines of familiar objects on construction paper or tagboard. Direct children to fill in the outlines with all kinds and colors of scraps from the "good stuff" box.

Glue styrofoam squiggles inside the outline of a sheep drawn on blue construction paper, a pig drawn on brown construction paper, or a bunny rabbit drawn on green construction paper. Encourage children to make up stories or poems to go with the squiggle art.

Create a fake kitchen menagerie. Provide clay, toothpicks, paper bags, individual serving-size cereal boxes, cups, etc., for the construction of imitation fruits and vegetables which can be made into animals. Then select scraps of all kinds from the "good stuff" box to give the finishing touches.

Don't forget to make use of those marvelous wallpaper sample books, free for the asking in many stores if you tell them they are for children's use. Wallpaper mountings make children's artwork fit for hanging in a gallery.

Make puppets from half-pint milk cartons. Flatten top and cut three sides through the middle. Add a construction paper tongue that sticks out to make a dragon for an original puppet script.

Make individual mail boxes from half-gallon milk cartons (also great for Valentine boxes).

Wash half-pint or pint milk cartons well and decorate them with paper strips or tempera paint to make decorative planters. Fill with soil and plant a budding pansy, begonia, or other blooming plant as a gift for a lucky recipient's windowsill. If time permits, seeds may be planted, tended, and observed instead.

Hold up an unusual box, and ask children to think of as many ways as possible to use it. List the ways on a chart.

Use corrugated boxes to make large paper animals that stand up. Draw and/or glue on features (ears, tails, facial features, etc.).

Make an "All About Me" cube. Cover the six sides of a small box with pictures cut from magazines or ones drawn by the child to tell about him- or herself. This makes a marvelous gift on Mother's Day, Father's Day, or Grandparent's Day!

Make binoculars from two toilet tissue rolls. Paint them black, glue them together, and attach a string to hang the binoculars around neck. Make nighttime pictures by cutting shapes (stars, moon, etc.) from foil and gluing them onto black construction paper.

Cut 9" x 12" placemats from scraps of solid, pastel-colored sheets. Let children use wax crayons to design "special person" placemats for someone they love. Press each mat between wax paper with a hot iron to seal colors.

Give each child a large outline picture on oak tag, a large-eyed blunt needle, and yarn with instructions to sew around the outline or fill in the picture.

Make Name Puzzles. Write each child's name with a marker on oak tag, and cut all letters apart as for a puzzle. Let each child put his or her own name together.

Make a variety of card pairs showing geometric designs, and make pairs of candy canes with different designs. Place these in a learning center setting for children to match during free time.

Use this recipe to make play-clay people. Roll dough about ¼" thick and use cookie cutters to cut basic shapes or help children make their own shapes. Roll small pieces of dough for eyes, cheeks, etc. Moisten with water to attach, and poke a hole at the top to thread. Bake at 325° until light brown, or air dry for 48 hours. Varnish to protect from moisture.

NO-COOK PLAY DOUGH

2 cups self-rising flour
2 Tablespoons alum
2 Tablespoons salt
2 Tablespoons cooking oil
1¼ cups boiling water

Add a touch of food coloring if desired. Mix, knead, and store in a covered container.